50+

Year Old

Entrepreneurs

Fulfilling Your Dreams In Your
Golden Years.
It's Never Too Late!

Peter Osalor

Published by:

POSAG International Ltd 9 Greenwich Quay London SE8 3EY

For comments or enquiries e-mail:

info@posagconsulting.com ISBN

978-0-957330-50-4

CONTENTS PAGE

PREFACE

Entrepreneurship is and always has been a passion of mine. I grew up in a family that did not have very much at all. Poverty was something that I experienced but success was something I desired to attain. 50+ Year Old Entrepreneurs has been written to encourage those that may have tried in the past and failed; it is also for those that are approaching the age of retirement. It is never too late to start again and it's never too late to begin an entrepreneurial journey. It is no secret that poverty and lack bring shame. Prosperity and success do the opposite. Money is a tool that can be used for good if used correctly. Money presents us with options and choices; the lack of money often takes away our ability to choose. You may have spent the majority of your working life with little options or have very rarely been given the power to choose. Being your own boss positions you to whole-heartedly take each opportunity that comes your way.

As an entrepreneur you can have a generational influence, both financially and otherwise, by setting up and running a successful business. A successful person is a person in authority and as you embark upon your entrepreneurial journey you will find yourself in a position of influence and notoriety. We all know the saying "show me your friends and I will show you who you are"; the same is true for money. What do you do with the cash that comes into your hands? The advantage of having lived for a while, experiencing seasons of lack and seasons where you want for nothing, is that the value of money takes on a different meaning.

Money is not *the* source, it is only a resource used to acquire the tangible things we desire in life. When starting my first businesses I did not get everything right. I failed at some things and after having spent some time building a global empire I found myself fighting bankruptcy and starting over. I was older, wiser and had learned a few lessons the second time round. As the saying goes, "age is nothing but a number" and this time round, my age and experience worked in my favour.

Regarding business, your age can be used to your advantage as you bring the skills and experiences you have acquired and pour them into your own business ventures. It is important to remember that no matter the amount of money you have you are never empty handed. Think about what is in your hand. By this I mean; think about your skills, your experience, the lessons you have learnt in life, the talents you possess and the things that come naturally or easily to you. These are all invaluable assets – they are priceless in comparison to the numerable worth of any amount of money. Would you rather have an apple or an apple tree? One will satisfy you temporarily and the other could serve as a valuable resource for a lifetime. This book will teach you how to see yourself as the apple tree and help you identify the strengths and talents you possess to run a successful business.

Entrepreneurialism is not merely about making money. It is about security and fulfillment, living a life where work is something that you look forward to and not simply endure. A successful entrepreneur is one that fulfils their goals, plans and purpose in life. They are progressive and resilient with clear concise objectives. The only person who can stop you is you – so why not read on? You are the vehicle that will bring success your way. The primary reason for life's potential of optimal accomplishment on earth is living a life that impacts humanity. True success is living a valuable and profitable life when benefits extend far beyond self – true success is leaving a legacy. Think about your children, your grandchildren, your family and friends. Successful living should be a generational role model. I am certain that if asked, you would say you desire to live a life of minimal regrets and sorrow. It is possible to do this by living a life that is progressive, not heading towards one destination, but continuously on a journey of discovery and development; fully maximizing life's opportunities towards the benefit of humanity.

Successful living entails that your presence is felt and your absence is noticed on earth, leaving a legacy or vacancy on earth when the time comes. If you can enlarge your vision then you will enlarge your business and your ability to succeed. Diligence and consistency are the keys to the greatness of an entrepreneur; you must maximize your time, a studious life provides steady success. As you continue to read I will show you how to study what other successful entrepreneurs have done so that you can follow suit.

I encourage you to no longer look at the word retirement as the end of a working career, nor look at your increasing age as a negative. See the season of retirement as the beginning, a new chapter on the road to a journey of entrepreneurial enlightenment. Let's begin to change the way we see the business world. This world is filled with limitless opportunities and it is up to us to ensure that we take those that are presented before us. Anyone can start a business but it takes someone with an entrepreneurial mind-set to successfully maintain a productive and lucrative one. The following pages provide many steps that, when followed, will lead you on the path to becoming a successful entrepreneur.

INTRODUCTION

Old age is golden they say, and the best time to enjoy the fruits of one's labour is in youth. Many times these fruits are either delayed or, due to circumstances, are lost for one reason or another. The benefit of hope is that it gives a reason to keep at it while awaiting desired outcomes. Old age is a time of life that can be viewed from two perspectives; as a half full glass or as a half empty one. A wise man once said age is in the mind - that is you are as old as your mind. The way a man looks at himself determines what he can achieve.

Retirement age is a period that can also be referred to as the 're-firing' age. There are more upsides to retirement periods than just laying back to shrivel up and die. On the contrary, it is a time that one should look forward to. Why? We will find out together as we explore the boundless opportunities that can be utilised to the benefit of the retiree. To start with, as a retiree, you must make a decision to refuse to live out the rest of your days in laziness or pure unbridled idleness. Instead, you can venture into a business of your own, doing something you enjoy doing day after day. Why not? You have the energy, the time and most likely the funds to start. As a workforce veteran, you bring a great deal to the table: maturity and a wide network of professional contacts and associates. With this in mind, if there is ever a time to get into the entrepreneurship race it is in retirement age. Whether for economic reasons or simply from a desire to remain active and relevant, or even a desire to try something new, self employment or business ownership is an attractive alternative to one's life career or work. This is mainly because it allows for lots of self-control over the type of work as well as time and finances.

50+ Year Old Entrepreneurs is designed for the purpose of encouraging and pushing you to the brink of your success and fulfillment in your retirement years. To begin with, make a list of the inhibitors you have to your dream of retiring well and simply put them aside. Yes, putting them aside being the operative words. In this book we are going to be discovering some of the secrets to revamping the second half of your life.

CHAPTER ONE

"The average person over 50 mentally pictures themselves as 15 years younger than they really are. People don't want to see who they really are. They want to see who they want to be."

Scott Gilbert, CEO Saatchi & Saatchi

RETIRING WELL - THE 50 YEAR OLDS AND OVER

In recent years, the meaning of retirement has come to change a lot. There has been an increase of individuals who belong to that class of the population who have taken the world by surprise as they have bounced back on their feet in the pursuit of business. Over two-thirds of retirees are active and enjoying a vigorous part of their life, more and more people are living longer and healthier lives and continuing to make positive and important contributions. You should too.

Retirement decisions vary from person to person but tend to be based on factors such as financial situations, responsibilities toward family members or health at retirement age. The idea of retiring used to be solely based on the pensions and benefits that are meant to accrue. Considering the fact that you cannot leave your job or paid employment as an inheritance for your children, you can however leave a business behind to be inherited; the time to start is now.

[1]**Emotional State of Retirees**

The results of a recent survey imply that most retirees have a positive attitude surrounding their retirement. According to the AIG SunAmerica Harris Interactive Reconditioning Retirements Survey, 95% of retirees believe themselves to be open-minded, while 94% think of themselves as both peaceful and independent. In retirement one major rule does apply and that is - have fun!

The state of mind and emotions which often characterizes retirement can be channelled positively for maximal results. When adequate plans were not put in place before exiting the workforce, the unprepared would feel dejected, uninterested, dissatisfied and sometimes have feelings of self-defeat. Others exhibited traits of psychological fluctuation in terms anxiety,

---

1 www.soyouwanna.com

depression and emotional imbalance. On the other hand, the minority who were prepared for the future felt secure, confident, certain and looked forward to retirement with eagerness and ease hoping to enjoy the fruits of their labour.

There are different categories of retirement. Some are forced while others are age related.

Forced Retirement

While many people plan, sometimes years in advance, when and how they will retire, others are forced into retirement through other circumstances. People who are forced to retire because of layoffs, the needs of family members or their own failing health often find retirement to be a difficult transition. Whatever one feels about his job, retirement, whether voluntary or mandatorily is inevitable.

Retirement can be devastating psychologically, because of the uncertainty of their retirement benefits. Others tend to feel really low and dejected because their skills may become obsolete through lack of use.

Some people started out their businesses when it seemed like there was no strength left in them, but soon their activities literally give them a new lease of life. Do you see a bleak future? It's probably because you have not set up anything to retire to, neither have you made any plans outside your retirement benefits to fall back on. There is a way out, and that is becoming self employed, or an entrepreneur if you will.

POPULATION

There are a high percentage of retirees all over the world; unfortunately, these people are classified as the dependent population. In 2002 7% of the world population was over 65 years old. Only 1% of the population of the United Arab Emirates was over 65 years old. China has the largest elderly population (92 million) but this is only 7% of the Chinese population. Growing proportions of elderly people are partly due to a result of people living longer and a number of fewer births, reducing the size of the younger population. Africa is home to only 6% of the world's population aged over 65.

Retirees are often considered as unproductive people and liabilities. This has to change if we are to make the best of the human resources that abound in this class of individuals. Age is not in any way a barrier to the level of input a person can give to himself or his family or even to society. It all starts in the mind.

Life expectancy in the world drops every year. Health issues as well as environmental issues are largely responsible for this. Nevertheless, individuals themselves are the ones who have the final say, so to speak, on how long or how well they wish to live. Finding your purpose or a passion and living it out is one way to ensure that you live a long and full life. This is not voodoo or clairvoyance, it is simply a fact that when life loses its appeal and lustre for a person, whether young old, they find it really hard to live for the next day. This is what getting back up in your retirement years can do for you; it can give you a new lease of life.

CHARACTERISTICS OF 50+ INDIVIDUALS

More time on their hands
Not in a hurry like the youth are Invaluable
experiences
Less family pressure
A strong sense of personal motivation to succeed More
flexible time
A new lease of life

Positive aspects of retirement

- A chance to start a new life. Whatever you have always wanted to try, now is the time to give it your best shot.

- Spending time with grandchildren is also wide open. Being retired gives you plenty of time to get to know your grandkids better.

- Travelling is also something many retirees do.

- Having an unstructured day is also a Godsend for many retirees. Without the constant push to work, work, work, some might see stress levels go down, along with improved health.

- Charity work is also a common activity amongst retirees. Since you no longer have to rely on a job for income, you have plenty of time to participate in activities that help your community and the world.

Potentials: According to Score, there has been an increasing number of Baby Boomers, people in their 50s and 60s, starting businesses. This makes sense considering the increasing lifespan of the elder community, the recession and its effects on retirement plans.

Hidden treasures abound in the senior population. One might wonder, isn't this a period of rest and just drifting on the wings of time till you pass on? Well, forgive me but I do not believe that is the way to go.

SOME NEGATIVE ASPECTS OF RETIREMENT

Fewer Job Opportunities

Individuals aged 45 years and older are more likely to face concealed age discrimination when attempting to change jobs or re-enter the work force. For many, retirement isn't quite what it used to be. As a workforce veteran, you bring a great deal to the table: maturity, strong finances and a wide network of professional contacts and associates.

Irregular Flow of Income

Even with the promise of pensions, which in most cases are either delayed or irregular. Being a retiree solely dependent on pensions and gratuity may not be a great idea as the flow of income, when irregular, may cause a lot hindrances for the retiree.

Redundancy

The feeling that is associated with 'rolelessness' is not pleasant and it may lead to bouts of depression for the retired person who was once full of zest for his or her job.

Dependency

Most retirees, due to the unreliable pension schemes in their countries or states, have to depend on their children for their upkeep. This can only be realistic when the children are able to cater for themselves as well as carry the additional burden of caring for their retired parents. In the absence of this much needed care, life becomes a lot harder and unpleasant for retirees.

Uncertainty of Future Plans

This uncertainty particularly crops up when there has been little or no fall back plans made by a retiree. The uncertainty that the future holds can be pretty scary. It may even lead to depression and lethargy among retired folks.

Economic Security

Earnings in retirement are usually small compared to the pre -retirement period for most retirees and health, status, nutrition, housing etc. are affected as a result.

Psychological Maladjustment

Psychological maladjustment results from severe loss of self esteem even when a new job is taken. Chances are the new job will pay less, leading to a drop in living standards. Also, the energy with which one is usually at their best will no longer be there.

CHAPTER TWO

WHAT DOES SELF-EMPLOYMENT ENTAIL FOR THOSE 50 YEARS +

Self-employment and entrepreneurship are one and the same, provided the self-employed person is willing to take the same risks as the entrepreneur. Many 50+ individuals have particular skills, knowledge and talents as well as experience, which could enable them to work for themselves. Self- employment as the name suggests is simply working for one's self. Being totally responsible to one's self as well as being able to exert control over one's time, frequency and input into the venture.

The truth is that many well-meaning individuals lose their enthusiasm and drive to be successfully self-employed in short order.

The concept of self-employment in this context is basically running your own business, not sub-contracting for instance, or consulting for one firm only. You are self-employed when you have several 'bosses' i.e. customers.

BENEFITS OF SELF-EMPLOYMENT

- Self-assuredness. You are able to use your own personal judgement and express your own ideas and opinions as you will have complete autonomy.

- Flexibility and control (over working hours). Imagine life without a commute, where you can adjust your work to your life - choose the hours and days you work and the time you finish - completely avoiding rush hour. If you can work from home, you can avoid commuting all together.

Independence

As a self-employed worker, you never have to jump through any administrative hoops to take your vacation time. In fact, with today's technology, you can work from a remote beach in the Caribbean or from your country home.

Self-fulfilment

The joy and satisfaction that comes from knowing that you can actually achieve what you set your heart to is a benefit of being self-employed that cannot be measured.

Realising a long held ambition

Self-employment gives you the creative freedom to strike out independently in your current field, or to make the career change you've been dreaming about for years.

Supplementing pension funds

There is potential for greater growth and earning because the more you work, the more you can make, which is not always true when you work for someone else.

Using skill or talents to a greater extent

The self-employed essentially have an unlimited earning potential rather than a set salary, all dependent on the work they put in.

Retire when you are ready

Being self-employed gives you the unreserved freedom to decide when you desire to retire from the business. On the contrary, as an employee, you either retire when you attain the specified age or forcefully.

Aside from the benefits that you accrue as an entrepreneur making the best of a second chance there are many wonderful benefits of entrepreneurship. Some of them are:

Providing employment to a huge mass of people; - people often hold a view that all those who do not get employed anywhere jump into entrepreneurship. This is contrary to the truth, entrepreneurship is not at all an encumbrance to an economy, rather it has been responsible for a huge percentage of employment opportunities. What's more is that approximately 34 million of fresh employment opportunities were created by entrepreneurs from the period of 1980. This data makes it clear that entrepreneurship heads a nation towards better opportunities, which is a significant input to an economy.

Contributing towards research and development systems;
- almost 2/3% of all innovations are due to entrepreneurs. Without the boom of inventions the world would have been a very dull place to live in. Inventions provide an easier way of getting things done through better and standardised technology.

Creates wealth for a nation and for individuals as well; - all individuals who search business opportunities usually, create wealth by entering into entrepreneurship. The wealth created, plays a considerable role in the development of a nation. The business as well as the entrepreneur contributes in some way or another to the economy, it may be in the form of products or services or boosting the GDP rates or tax contributions. The ideas, thoughts, and inventions are also a great help to the nation.

Sky-scraping heights of apparent prospects; - the individual gets maximum scope for growth and opportunity if he enters into entrepreneurship. He not only earns, he learns while he earns. This is a real motivating factor for any entrepreneur as the knowledge and skills he develops while owning his enterprise become assets for a lifetime which one usually lacks when a person is under employment. The individual goes through a grooming process when he becomes an entrepreneur. In this way it not only benefits him but also the economy as a whole.

It is a challenging opportunity for the people; - although entrepreneurship is a challenging task, in most cases the rewards it gives are much more than what one anticipates. It does not only reward an entrepreneur on financial levels but also on an individual level. It provides self-satisfaction to the entrepreneur.

Entrepreneurship provides self-sufficiency; - the entrepreneur not only becomes self-sufficient, entrepreneurship also provides great standards of living to its employees. It provides opportunities to a number of people working in the organisation. The basic factors, which become a cause of happiness, are liberty, monetary rewards and the feeling of contentment that one gets after doing the job. Therefore the contribution of entrepreneurs makes the economy an improved place to live in.

CHAPTER THREE

REASONS FOR STARTING YOUR OWN BUSINESS

Choosing to have another job after retirement is no longer uncommon. Some want to work for the satisfaction of accomplishing something. Others work to stay in touch with people. Some haven't developed hobbies or interests that occupy enough of their free time. Of course, as the world economies continue to struggle attempting to find another source of income is important to many of us especially retirees.

Below are some of the reasons you could have for starting your own business:

Money

The worry of not having enough to fall back on after retirement propels a lot of people to start up their own businesses. Whether you are nearing retirement or you are already retired, starting your own business may just be one way of increasing your income flow and allow you to grow your wealth too. Your focus is to meet the needs of your potential customers and money will come in.

Time

Retirees usually have a lot of time on their hands and this is a very vital requirement in order to start your own business. The reason is that you have the luxury of time to weigh your options, do some research, make informed decisions and have a hassle free business experience. Time also allows you to grow slowly step-by-step.

Experience

This is one gift that older people have that cannot really be quantified. As a retiree you have had diverse experiences of what customer service for instance is and what it is not. You can easily decide what step to take concerning certain aspects of your business and your life. You can also sense what people need and want, besides you of all people know what hard work is and you are not afraid to get your hands dirty.

Energy

Whether you retire at 50 or above or you just feel the need to branch off and start out on your own, there is an undeniable amount of mental energy you posses. Your mind is still as sharp as it was when you were much younger especially if you have been in active service in the last decade or more of your life. With all that energy, you can get up and get started if the idea of sitting around all day and doing nothing with your retirement period gets boring.

Control

Being self-employed during this age bracket is usually more rewarding for you. You get to exercise control over your time and resources as well as your rules and decisions. You can succeed or fail on your own terms based on the amount of time, resources, knowledge and passion you have put into the work.

Passion

If you lived most of your working life doing a job that did not excite you or perhaps you worked for a grumpy boss who was never satisfied and you never had the chance to let out your creative and fun side, well now that you are retired you have the chance to make the best of it; pursue your passion and get paid for it too.

ADVANTAGES OF STARTING YOUR BUSINESS AT 50+

[2]Older workers have some distinct advantages when it comes to running a small business. They also have some unique considerations that younger workers don't share. Here are just a few of the advantages of starting a business later in life.

1. Financial Stability

Generally, older workers have more financial resources than freshly minted college grads. They have a longer credit history and have typically built up more equity in a home, which can come in handy when setting up a business.

2. Contacts

If you've worked in a field related to the industry you wish to enter as a business owner, you probably have valuable contacts that can help you get started. Even if you are going into an unrelated field, you've built many relationships over the years that you can leverage as a new business owner.

3. Avoiding Age Discrimination

Despite federal laws prohibiting age discrimination in some countries, it still happens, and a laid-off older worker may have a hard time competing for jobs against younger workers. If you work for yourself, you don't have to worry about that. And if you're laid off from a company where you were employed for long-term, a severance package can serve as start-up capital.

---

2 www.legalzoom.com

4. Experience and Energy

You've learned a lot over the years, and even if you are entering an entirely new industry, some of your skill set will be transferable and many of the life lessons you have learnt will apply. That's an advantage. Also, people today are living longer, healthier lives than ever, so 50+ isn't necessarily the time to slow down. In fact, your most productive years could be ahead of you.

Another benefit is that many companies you do business with will respect your experience. Unlike younger entrepreneurs who have to build trust with companies due to their lack of work experience, you have a leg up over your younger competition since people associate age with experience.

CHAPTER FOUR

CHARACTERISTICS OF THE SELF-EMPLOYED

Entrepreneurs must be in a position to acquire the status of a trader, craftsman or self-employed intellectual worker and must be in possession of the required qualifications and permits for their activity.

[3]Personal Characteristics Needed for Self-Employment

Self-employment requires determination to stick with the program. Some find that it's too easy to slack off when there's no boss keeping track of production. An afternoon off here, a full day there and soon self-employment becomes unemployment.
Above all, to be successful, self-employed individuals must have self-discipline. These are the people who can operate
without supervision, who can keep themselves motivated, and
who don't give in to discouragement when things don't go as planned.

Many people wish to own their own business and become self-employed. Owning your own business requires a lot of work and dedication. This may be contrary to what many people think at first. Being motivated, persistent and patient are important traits to have. For success in owning a business, the things to keep in mind are responsibilities, resources and research. Being self-employed entails a lot of responsibility. Organisation, time management, budgeting, communication and discipline are just some of the characteristics needed for owning a business. In addition, asking for help is very important. When things get overwhelming, it is good to have assistance. Delegation can help to minimise your workload and bring forth more efficiency.

[4]Self Discipline

Do you recognise the difference between takings and profit? If takings make you feel rich and successful, or feel as though you have 'arrived', beware; failure is imminent! Profit is the

---

3 Self Employment @ Suite 101 www. suite101.com 4
www.howtobooks.co.uk

balance you are left with after all your expenses have been paid. Plan and budget: it is the only way to keep your head out of the clouds and focused on the future.

Total Commitment to Hard Work

You don't have to be a workaholic but you do need to understand that the working day of the average civil servant bears no relation to the working day of a self-employed businessperson neither does the relative stress level. On average the self-employed person works 35% longer. The plus side is that the self-employed person has no ceiling on their earnings.

Health

It's easy to overlook the importance of your health. Minor ailments sometimes go unnoticed, regular check-ups get cancelled or at the best postponed. If you want your car to give optimum performance you have to have it serviced. Your health is perhaps your most valuable asset - take care of it!

Determination

You'll need 'true grit'. Expect an abundance of crises. Set your goals but be ready to throw them to the wind. Self- employment is not for the faint hearted; forget the path of least resistance. Follow your plan but build in a degree of flexibility.

Enthusiasm

If you have employees, inject them with your enthusiasm - you will be amazed at the result. If you can get them to own the vision you have for your business and personalise it then your goals and aims will be equally important to them because your passions will be united under the same vision.

Judgement

Can you make a decision or do you drag your feet? Do you have the ability to sum up a situation, make a decision and stick to it? You can and should consult others, but at the end of the day, it's down to you. Don't be a fence sitter. Make a decision. It may be the wrong one but next time you will be speaking from experience.

Integrity

Customers must believe your word is your bond: suppliers must believe the same. How many times have you personally experienced someone cancelling an appointment, or worse, not showing up? Do you reorder? Of course not! Don't make the same mistake in your business; your clientele will grow if you are a person that keeps your word.

Asking for help

Don't be afraid to ask for advice. If the man in your favourite coffee shop keeps his staff and you don't, ask him how he does it. He will be flattered and you will be wiser.

[5]You have to be flexible to be self-employed

If you start a business, you no longer have "one" job with clearly defined duties and responsibilities. You'll suddenly have multiple jobs, which will be often interrupted by unforeseen crises (particularly in the start up phase). Many employees are used to having days filled with predictable activities; many self-employed people don't.

And once you start a business, there's nowhere to pass the buck. As an employee, you may be used to passing problems up along the food chain or not be very involved in decision- making. As a self-employed business owner, you're the one

---

5 Susan Ward About.com Guide. 6 Traits You Need to Move From Being an Employee to Being Self-Employed

34

who will have to deal with whatever the crisis is and solve the problem. You're the one who will have to make the decisions.

You have to be a self-motivated initiator

When you're an employee, other people tell you what to do, either directly or indirectly. You get used to having your actions directed by others. But you have to direct your own actions as a small business owner. You can't just sit there and hope that maybe some clients will stroll in or that someone will drop by out of the blue with inventory for your retail store. No one's going to drop work on your desk or point out what needs to be done. For many people who try to become self-employed and start businesses after having a long-term full-time job, this is the hardest adjustment to make.

You have to be able to recognise opportunities and go after them

Most employees do what they're assigned to do. If you start a business, you need to be the one constantly watching for opportunities - and be able to recognise them when you see them. It might be a small opportunity, such as the chance to pick up a new client, or a large one, such as getting your product on the shelves in a large retail chain, but as a small business owner, you have to keep scanning the horizon yourself and positioning yourself to benefit from the opportunities that you find. As an employee, you may be used to operating in a "head-down" position; if you're going to start a business and become successfully self-employed, you need to start operating in the "head-up" position.

When you're self-employed, you have to be able to plan ahead

Your last job may have involved no planning at all, as that was someone else's job. Or perhaps your job involved planning on a localised level, such as planning a particular project. If you want to start a business, you need to develop expertise in both short-term and long-range planning; it's about to become a big part of your life.

When you start a business, one of your first tasks will be to work through a business plan. As your business becomes operational, you'll find that your plan (however detailed) needs to be revised and that other plans need to be created, as you work towards the long-range goals that you've set for your business. From following someone else's plan as an employee, you have to learn how to create the plans yourself - and adapt the plans to changing circumstances.

You need to be prepared to put in a constant and consistent effort

We've all seen employees who are just going through the motions, or who are just "putting in the time" until retirement. You don't need to be a co-worker to know who these people are. As a customer or client you can tell, too. Bluntly, starting a business takes energy and you need to be able to give it 100%. You can't afford to just coast along, or go through the motions, if you're running a business. Your customer and/or clients need to know that you are devoting 100% of your talent, skill and attention to them - they will go elsewhere if they don't feel this is the case.

You need to deliver this constant and consistent effort without the employee safety net. Many employees are used to being able to "call in sick" and have someone else cover their job, for instance. As a self-employed business owner, you'll have to go in and give it your best effort no matter how you feel or close up shop if you don't have employees who can fill in. You can also say goodbye to the holidays that many employees enjoy, both the annual number of weeks and the statutory holidays, at least until your business is established to the point that you can manage your own time.

You have to be able to deal with uncertainty

As a self-employed entrepreneur, there's no guarantee that the products or services you offer will be in demand six months from now. There's no guarantee that your customers will pay their bills on time or even pay them at all. There's no guarantee that your current big client, who seems to be perfectly happy with your work, won't drop you next week. There's actually no guarantee that you will make any income this month or the month after. For many ex-employees who are used to having a pay cheque arrive regularly every two weeks, the uncertainty of being self-employed is very difficult to deal with.

Are you still asking, "How do I start a business?" Good! Because the point of this chapter is not to scare you off, but to make you aware of how you have to readjust your thinking to make the transition from employee or retiree to self-employed business owner. Hopefully as you read through the list of traits you need to become successfully self-employed, you were saying to yourself, "I can do this". Because every one of the traits listed is an attitude or behaviour that can be learned, and when it comes to being self-employed, awareness is more than half the battle.

Now that you know that you're the kind of person who can start a business and run it successfully, where do you go from here?

CHAPTER FIVE

HOW TO BECOME SELF-EMPLOYED

PRACTICAL STEPS

- **Develop an interest in owning a business**: The very first step towards achieving any feat is having a desire or an interest. It is your interest that fuels the passion you need to get your business running and thriving. Don't jump into a business because everyone around you is doing it. This is what creates a glut in the market and a reduction in customer demand. Instead, find out what drives and motivates you. This is what will set you apart from your competition and keep you going when things get tough.

- **Ideas/ Need**: To start a business you need to conceptualise what you want to venture into. There are two major ways to streamline this; either through an idea you have thought out or simply through a need you have noticed in your immediate environment. There are certain situations you notice which make you most uncomfortable and which you desire strongly to correct. That could be a pointer to what you should build your new business around. For instance, a littered street or community, lack of power supply, child labourers, home deliveries for groceries etc. At the end of this book, there are about 50 business ideas that you could choose from to launch your entrepreneurial journey.

- **Write it down**: It has been proven that the faintest pen is stronger than the strongest memory. Writing your ideas and goals down commits you, to a large extent, to stick to achieving them. Writing down and keeping your goals where you can see them every day, is the first major step to cross on the road to accomplishing these goals. Dividing them into short, medium and long term goals will better help put these goals into perspective and further aids in making seemingly insurmountable targets become easier to accomplish. It is advisable and quite practicable to carry a notepad around as you go about your daily activities. This way whenever the inspiration for an idea comes into your mind, you can write it down before it slips out of your mind.

- **Get a team**: Most times, people fail in their attempt to start a business when they try to handle all the aspects of the start up by themselves without engaging help from others when necessary. The temptation to carry the burden all by one's self, in order to save money is very strong as every new entrepreneur tries to save as much as is possible. This could be a death trap for a young business especially one that involves processes. It is wise to engage the help of others when and where it is expedient that you do so.

- **Get started**: The fastest way to start your business is to just start. Breaking the initial inertia and launching out is the only way to get going and get ahead. Saying it without backing it up with actions will only leave it in the realm of wishful thinking.

- **Re-evaluate and re-launch**: Over a period of time, preferably three months after your start up, it is advised that you take a retreat and re-assess your business. Check for pitfalls, set backs or even failures you have experienced within that period of time. If peradventure you have not experienced any of these, it is still quite necessary that you take a step back, review your performance and make adjustments where you deem fit.

- **Get some sort of training**: Having the interest is not enough. You need to get some sort of formal training, either by studying articles, books, newsletters or watching programs that teach you how to start and run a business effectively; or via an apprenticeship. Just as a tailor learns by apprenticing herself to an established tailor, find someone who has a similar business to yours and learn from them. One admonition, don't expect to learn everything you need to do in your own business from someone else; you are unique and you should let it show as you conduct your business in a way that is unique to you.

- **Carry out self-assessment/analysis:** What do you like to do and what would you rather someone else does for you? It is important to consider your strengths and weaknesses, temperament, personality and other factors when starting a business. You want to start a business that compliments your personality not one that cramps your style.

- **Generate possible business ideas:** One great entrepreneur, Linus Pauling, once said that "the best way to have a good idea is to have lots of ideas." Brainstorm with family or friends what ideas are out there for a good business. This will generate many results, most of which you will discard. Pick the one that aligns most with your passion and personality. If you are one of those chronic procrastinators and you have ideas but have not taken any concrete steps to start your own business, it is time to do so. On the other hand, if your family and friends do not provide ideas that resonate with your passion, you may be wondering where to find better ideas.

Here are some tips:

1. Write out what is on your mind. Whether you will ultimately discard these initial ideas is not the problem; discover them first before you criticise. The more ideas you start with, the better.

2. If your mind is blank or you do not have the faintest

idea of what business to go into, then you should try asking yourself some questions such as:

- **What education have you received?**
- **What inspires you?**
- **What skills do you possess?**
- **What are your talents?**
- **What do people praise you for doing?**
- **What past or present career positions provide you with work experience you can use?**

Your ability to answer these questions will reveal to you, your personal business assets. Then write down a list of some goods and services that can be created and sold from them. Also you may not generate an idea, but you can see a need and work towards filling it; that is, take advantage of opportunities. In generating ideas, remember that anything you can do well could be turned into a business.

CHAPTER SIX

SELF-EMPLOYMENT AND ENTREPRENEURSHIP

Some schools of thought believe that there is a wide difference between a self-employed person and an entrepreneur. There are some striking similarities that both concepts share which makes them more similar than different.

SIMILARITIES BETWEEN A SELF-EMPLOYED PERSON AND AN ENTREPRENEUR

There are basic similarities between entrepreneurs and self-employed people. The same fundamental principles of success apply in business whether it is a small scale business or a franchise.

1. Confidence

[6]This is a hallmark of the entrepreneur. Not all of us are born with confidence, but that does not mean we are not capable of it. Many confident women and men gain their sense of self esteem and faith in their ability to greet challenges by acting – even when they lack the confidence – and then gain strength and belief in themselves by seeing the results and gaining the praise and respect of others.

2. Sense of Ownership

Acting like an owner means taking responsibility for getting things done and doing them with care and attention. Rather than viewing a problem as someone else's, the entrepreneur sees it as his or her own and takes pride in finding a solution, leaving things in better shape than they were before encountering them, and improving upon situations rather than leaving them unattended. While a sense of ownership makes for a stellar employee, the entrepreneur knows that the goal is not to be owned by the enslavement of too much responsibility.

---

6 www.actioncoach.com

3. Communication

Entrepreneurs recognise that the most important part of any business is the human element. Human resources – whether in the form of clients, employees, or strategic partners – are what make or break a business; and communication is the key to successful relationships with people. The entrepreneur works to hone communication skills, whether those are written, spoken, or non-verbal messages conveyed through body language. And to support communication, he or she will take advantage of all available tools and resources. Those might include foreign language or public speaking classes, computer and telecom technology, search engine optimisation or Neurolinguistic Programming (NLP) as it relates to sales and marketing, or specialised writing such as that needed for grants, business proposals, mission statements, or policy manuals. Above all, the entrepreneur develops a keen ability to listen and hear what others are trying to say, because the best communicators started off by first being the best listeners.

4. Passionate about Learning

Entrepreneurs are often "autodidactic" learners, which means that much of what they know they learned not in a formal classroom setting but instead on their own by seeking out information, asking questions and conducting personal reading and research. They also are quick to learn from their own mistakes, which means they are less prone to keep repeating them due to arrogance, ego, or a blindness to one's own faults, shortcomings, or errors in judgement. To teach is to learn. And in order to lead, train and impart experience to others the entrepreneur is constantly striving to learn more and be better educated. Because of the passion for education, true entrepreneurs surround themselves with people who either know more than they do or know things that are different from what they know.

They entertain the views of others and perspectives that may be unlike their own, for instance, in order to be better students of human nature. In this way they continue to enrich themselves with knowledge while also making a concerted effort to grow that knowledge by sharing it with others who are also front row students of life's valuable and unlimited lessons.

5. Team Player

Those who go into business for themselves but do not utilise teamwork wind up without the team but still have all the work to get done. They shoulder the whole burden for themselves, and wind up just trading their old job for a new and more demanding one – in an attempt to be self-employed. But the new venture carries greater personal and financial risks. On the other hand, team players know how to succeed by employing the physics of interpersonal synergy and dynamic relationships. One twig can be easily snapped, but a bundle of small twigs becomes stronger than the sum of its individual parts and can be impossible to bend, much less break. The same goes for businesses, and successful entrepreneurs leverage teamwork to get the heavy lifting done without breaking stride.

6. System-Oriented

Like mathematical formulas, good systems allow us to reproduce great results every time – with less and less exertion of energy or resources. Entrepreneurs rely upon systems before they rely upon people and they look for system based solutions before searching for human resource solutions. If a person gets the job done but falls sick or leaves, the results of the job are threatened. But if a system is created to get the job done, anyone can step in and follow the blueprint to get the desired result. Similarly, when troubleshooting and problem solving, the entrepreneur will first examine and study the system – because a flaw in the system will produce a flawed outcome each and every time.

Designing, implementing, and perfecting systems is one of the most useful and rewarding skills of an entrepreneur.

7. Dedicated

Entrepreneurs dedicate themselves to the fulfilment of their plans, visions, and dreams, and that tenacity of purpose generates electricity throughout the whole organisation. One of the biggest reasons that companies fail is because they lose focus. Target a goal, clarify the objective, refine the brand, and narrow the margin of error. Regardless of what the effort might involve, an entrepreneur brings a single-minded dedication to the task by being committed to a positive outcome and ready and willing to do the needful. No matter what that might mean in terms of rising to meet a challenge or acting above and beyond the call of duty, the entrepreneur shows steadfast dedication.

8. Grateful

Being grateful for what we have opens us up to receive more. A reason why that is true is because those who are grateful appreciate what they are given. They respect and nurture things they are given or made responsible for. They do their best to make things grow instead of allowing them to dwindle away due to neglect. Entrepreneurs learn to take nothing for granted in this world. That gives them the agility and flexibility to adapt to changes and demands, while it also invests in them a thankfulness that reminds them that riches and wealth are not about "stuff", but are about fulfilment, satisfaction and the pleasure that comes from one's accomplishments and contributions.

9. Optimistic

A positive outlook is essential for the entrepreneur, who learns to see setbacks as bargain priced tuition for valuable business lessons gained through firsthand experience. Past shortcomings, failures, or disappointments are relegated to the past so that they cannot continue to haunt the present or obstruct the future. And when things go right and the business prospers, this further fuels the optimism and positive mindset of an entrepreneur, helping to give impetus and momentum for greater accomplishments and increased hopefulness.

10. Gregarious

Because business is all about people, entrepreneurs tend to be socially outgoing. They get excited about sharing ideas, products and services; and that excitement becomes contagious amongst their employees, clients, friends, and other contacts both within and beyond the business sphere. But women and men who work hard as entrepreneurs also relish the unique opportunity to have fun doing something that they love as their primary vocation. Human resource experts, career counsellors and business psychologists all agree that those who do jobs they enjoy and are good at have higher rates of success and broader measures of satisfaction. Entrepreneurs know that firsthand, from their own experience, and they tend to be fun-loving people both on and off the job.

11. Leader by Example

Entrepreneurs not only lead themselves through self- motivation as self-starters who jump into tasks with enthusiasm, but they are also skilled at leading others. They know the importance of teamwork, and they understand the need to appreciate others, support them and reward them accordingly. True leaders do not become indispensable, otherwise things fall apart in their absence and they can never rise to the highest level of entrepreneurial freedom and prosperity. Neither do they squander the potential of those working under their guidance. As renowned business consultant and retired United States Air Force Major General Perry M. Smith once wrote, "Leaders who share their power and their time can accomplish extraordinary things. The best leaders understand that leadership is the liberation of talent; hence they gain power not only by constantly giving it away, but also by not grabbing it back."

12. Not Afraid of Risk or Success

Many people would be successful if they only took chances. And many people who do take chances and become somewhat successful find the realisation of their dreams an overwhelming possibility, so they sabotage their continued success by retreating back into a comfort zone of smallness. As discussed earlier, the employee mindset is preoccupied with a need for security. Those who cling to what is familiar to them – even if it means the denial of their dreams – lack the perseverance and ambition that the real entrepreneur exhibits. Entrepreneurs are not immune to fear. But they prioritise their approach to life so that the fear of failure, frustration, boredom, drudgery and dissatisfaction far outweighs the lingering fear of success. Entrepreneurs also share an emotional trait - optimism. Being negative and pessimistic about things just does not get you anywhere.

TYPES OF SELF-EMPLOYMENT

When you become self-employed it means you are working on your own business rather than working for an employer and there are a number of things to take into consideration. Working for yourself can have a number of advantages and disadvantages. For example, it means you are in control of what you do, so you can organise your own hours. On the other hand, it can involve working very hard and you may no longer have a regular income.

When you start a business you can do so either as a **sole trader, partnership** or **limited company.** The type of structure you choose depends on the kind of business you are embarking on, whom you will be doing business with and your attitude towards risk.

Setting up as a **sole trader** involves you setting up a business

51

on your own. There is no division between business assets or personal assets, which include your share of any assets jointly owned with another person (such as your house or car). Your liability is unlimited which means that personal assets can be used to pay business debts.

[7]A **partnership** is a type of unincorporated business organisation in which multiple individuals, called general partners, manage the business and are equally liable for its debts; other individuals called limited partners may invest but not be directly involved in management and are liable only to the extent of their investments. Unlike a **Limited Liability Company** or a corporation, in a partnership each partner shares equal responsibility for the company's profits and losses, and its debts and liabilities. The partnership itself does not pay income taxes, but each partner has to report their share of business profits or losses on their individual tax return.

[8]A **Limited Liability Company** (LLC) is a flexible form of enterprise that blends elements of partnership and corporate structures. It is a hybrid business entity having certain characteristics of both a corporation and a partnership or sole proprietorship (depending on how many owners there are).

There are two main types of self-employment. One is obviously home-based and may involve some type of computer work. Another type of work, however, requires one to actually own and operate a business. The business may be home-based, but just as often is not. One may work out of a van, an office or building situated somewhere other than the home, such as a retail store, or one may offer services and skills, such as housekeeping skills, horse training, sewing, etc.

7 http://www.investorwords.com
8 http://en.wikipedia.org

Self-employment, especially for the 50+, entails the following and more:

- Producing something
- Selling the product or service to customers or clients
- Planning spending and income generation
- Registering the business with the appropriate authorities
- Possibly borrowing money to run the business
- Possibly employing other people or finding a business partner

Schumpeter tied entrepreneurship to the creation of five basic "new combinations."

- Introduction of a new good
- Introduction of a new method of production
- The opening of a new market
- The conquest of a new source of supply
- The carrying out of a new organisation of industry

Is Starting a Business Right for You?

Starting a business at any age is a risk. When you're your own boss, you are solely responsible for paying your taxes, putting aside money for the future and providing your own health care coverage. But the bottom line is that age should never be a deterrent. For millions of American entrepreneurs who are 50 and older, owning a business is a highly rewarding alternative to the daily grind, and to retirement.

CHAPTER SEVEN

YOU ARE AN ENTREPRENEUR

In a State of the Union address, President Obama reiterated the importance of entrepreneurs and praised their determination especially in this economy: "We should start where most new jobs do - in small businesses, companies that begin when an entrepreneur takes a chance on a dream, or a worker decides it's time she became her own boss." An entrepreneur is a man or woman who is driven to establish a business to take advantage of the financial opportunities and personal fulfilment offered by pursuing their own dreams and shaping their own destiny in local, national, and global economies.

What is entrepreneurship?

Entrepreneurship has always been an important part of the economic tradition of many wealthy countries. Generally speaking, entrepreneurship refers to the creation or expansion of new businesses and industries, often by individuals who perceive a new market niche or opportunity and assume the risk of the venture.

TIPS AND SUGGESTIONS FOR ENTREPRENEURS

There is an increasing trend of entrepreneurship as senior citizens are becoming interested in starting their own business and being their own boss. It has also been noted that older entrepreneurs, in their passion and desire to accomplish and fulfill big dreams, are ignoring certain factors, taking things too fast and rushing into new ventures without enough training or proper planning. As a result they face serious challenges and issues. Entrepreneurs whether young or old should consider several factors and elements before starting any venture. Some of the important and useful tips are as follows:

- Go for what you love and are passionate about

- Have proper direction and know what you want

- Think out of the box and come up with radical and non-traditional ideas

- You should follow the rules

- Use the resources gathered and developed during your youth and working years

- Look to a mentor for proper guidance

- Make most of the online resources

- Establish proper, realistic, and well thought plans, strategies, and targets

- Have confidence in yourself and your ideas

The place to start when thinking about starting your own business is getting to know yourself. Do you have the personality to run a successful business? Are you a leader? Do you connect well with people? Complete the Entrepreneur Quiz in Appendix 1 to find out how well your personality fits into an entrepreneurial mindset. Be truthful. If it appears you don't have an entrepreneurial mindset, you can always grow one and this book will move you towards that goal.

PITFALLS TO AVOID WHEN STARTING YOUR BUSINESS

Though your business is unique to you, it is not so unique that you cannot find similarities with other businesses. For starters, the basic objective of any business enterprise is to make money. Thus, it is how you plan to make money that differs. The following are some errors people in business make that you should strive to avoid:

- Not listening to those who know the ropes

It is important to believe in yourself when starting your business, but don't become too self-assured. One of the most humbling realisations is that you do not have all the answers! Seek out professionals such as lawyers that can help you deal with some of the technical aspects of your business. It is also wise to seek out individuals directly involved in your industry who can provide insights into the operation of your business and the demographics of your clientele.

- Lacking a business plan

As we stated earlier, your business plan will provide you with a blueprint for your idea. Sure, you can run a business without ever writing out a plan, however, a plan helps you see the big picture, plan for contingencies and obtain funding. Your business will be better off with a plan. On the other hand, don't get so caught up in writing a business plan that you never get round to putting the plan into action.

- Lack of funding

Inadequate planning may lead to lack of funding for start up or expansion. It may also lead to a lack of adequate financial savings to cushion inevitable rough spots in a business cycle.

- Situating your business in a bad spot

All business owners should find a location that is both easily accessible and highly visible to potential clientele. When picking out your site, keep in mind the changing needs of you and your customers, the possible addition of competitors to your area, and the image the surrounding businesses project. Also consider the duration of each lease you are asked to begin or renew.

- Fear

Perhaps the single most destructive force to any business venture is fear. If you are afraid to take risks, you will never succeed in your business. You must let go of excuses, procrastination and doubt in order to achieve business success. Don't make a habit of postponing what you know needs to be done just because you are afraid to take a bold step. As the saying goes, nothing ventured, nothing gained.

CHAPTER EIGHT

Men do not quit playing because they grow old; they grow old because they quit playing.

Oliver Wendell Holmes

PEOPLE THAT STARTED THEIR BUSINESSES AT 50 AND ABOVE

The key to successful entrepreneurship is simply doing it. Regardless of age or circumstance, when the opportunity presents itself, you must go for it. Here are the stories of five "golden year entrepreneurs", who have effectively made gold for themselves. There are some startling statistics about entrepreneurs across the world that gives us an insight into what the entrepreneurial climate is like. This is demonstrated by a recent report from the Kauffman foundation for entrepreneurship. The report is titled "The Anatomy of an Entrepreneur". It's based on a survey of 549 company founders across a variety of industries.

1. The average and median age of company founders when they started their current companies was 40.

2. 95.1 per cent of respondents themselves had earned bachelor's degrees, and 47 per cent had more advanced degrees.

3. Less than 1 per cent came from extremely rich or extremely poor backgrounds.

4. 15.2 per cent of founders had a sibling that previously started a business.

5. 69.9 per cent of respondents indicated they were married when they launched their first business. An additional 5.2 per cent were divorced, separated, or widowed.

6. 59.7 per cent of respondents indicated they had at least one child when they launched their first business, and 43.5 per cent had two or more children.

7. 74.8 per cent indicated a desire to build wealth as an important motivation in becoming an entrepreneur.

8. Only 4.5 per cent said the inability to find traditional employment was an important factor in starting a business.

9. Entrepreneurs are usually better educated than their parents.

10. Entrepreneurship doesn't always run in the family. More than half (51.9 per cent) of respondents were the first in their families to launch a business.

11. The majority of respondents (75.4 per cent) had worked as employees at other companies for more than six years before launching their own companies.

These statistics only go to show that whatever peculiar situation you may find yourself in, should not pose a hindrance to your launching out and making the best of the rest of your life. Below are examples of entrepreneurs who have made their mark on the world by striving against all odds to succeed in their chosen paths in business. They all have one common denominator, they are senior citizens just like you.

1. Jack Weil, Founder of Rockmount

Jack A. Weil passed away on August 13, 2008 at the age of 107. The fact that he lived to the ripe old age of 107 is impressive. The fact that he was still the chief executive of the company he founded and working 40 plus hours a week until his final days is simply amazing. In 1946, he formed Rockmount, a western high fashion clothing retailer that continues to manufacturer it's shirts in the US after many competitors moved offshore. Achieving historical fame, various accounts state Mr. Weil either invented the modern bolo tie or named it. His secret to heath, wealth and happiness? "He loved his work."

2. Poppy Bridger, Owner of Anaheim Test Labs

After working as a PhD chemist for 45 years, Poppy Bridger, retired at the age of 69 to care for her ailing mother. But her 72nd birthday gift was an opportunity to buy and operate the lab she had worked at. With about $250K in savings, back to work she went!
On any given day, you will find Bridger testing the authenticity of a precious heirloom or analysing the properties of metal fatigue. To help with the growing work load at the lab, she has subsequently hired her son and daughter to work with her.
She goes to work every day, and at the age of 84 is bringing into the business about $350K annually.

3. Colonel Harland Sanders, Founder of Kentucky Fried Chicken

The world famous Colonel Sanders launched his business at the age of 65, using his first Social Security check as start up funds. A master of personal branding, Sanders leveraged his honorary "Colonel" title and constantly wore the stereotypical "southern gentleman" white-suit and black tie. The rocket like growth of KFC is now legendary, and prior to his death Colonel Sanders' restaurant chain had opened over 6,000 locations with sales of more than $2 billion.
During his entrepreneurial tenure Sanders met with the U.S. Congressional Committee of Ageing and spoke against mandatory retirement, highlighting the love for work and the value of wisdom in the work place.

4. Sylvia Lieberman, Creator of Archibald Mouse Books

Sylvia Lieberman became an entrepreneur in the autumn of 2007 when she was 90. This was when she realised her dream of having her first children's book published. She decided to start a company to author and promote the book.

Archibald's Swiss Cheese Mountain is an award-winning book about a little mouse with a big heart who teaches children how to reach their big dreams. Not only is Lieberman an entrepreneur, but a philanthropic one! A portion of the proceeds goes to two children's charities.

Despite her age, Sylvia works tirelessly promoting her book at book-signings and readings, TV appearances, radio and print interviews and she even appeared on a float in a parade. And all these efforts increase the amount she donates to charities.

5. Barbara Miller, Founder of Miller Paper Company

Being an entrepreneur was never really a consideration in Barbara Miller's life. After quitting her job in the paper industry after 30 years of service, she assumed she was done. But as she packed her stuff, her former colleagues begged her to start a new business... so she did. In January of 1995, Miller opened the doors to Miller Paper Company and started with $300K in savings and 15 employees. Business has not been a walk in the park, to say the least. Miller started her company and was immediately sued by her former employer. A few months later she struggled with ovarian cancer.

Today the business is generating over $7M in annual revenue and has been on D&B's list of the nation's fastest growing companies.

6. [9]Mary Kay Ash

Mary Kay Ash, born Mary Kathlyn Wagner married Ben Rogers at age 17. While her husband served in World War II, she sold books door-to-door. After her divorce in 1945, Ash went to work for Stanley Home Products. Frustrated when passed over for a promotion in favour of a man that she had trained, Ash retired in 1963 and intended to write a book to assist women in business. The book turned into a business plan for her ideal company, and in the summer of 1963, Mary

9 Wikipedia.org   http://en.wikipedia.org/wiki/Mary_Kay_Ash

Kay Ash and her new husband, George Arthur Hallenbeck, began Mary Kay Cosmetics with a $5,000 investment. She considered the Golden Rule, the founding principle of Mary Kay Cosmetics, and the company's marketing plan was designed to allow women to advance by helping others to succeed. She advocated "praising people to success" and her slogan "God first, family second, career third" expressed her insistence that the women in her company keep their lives in balance.

7. [10]McDonald's and Ray Kroc

McDonalds was started by Ray Kroc, when most people his age were retiring. Ray Kroc was 52 years old in 1954. He was a milk shake machine salesman. One day he happened on a hamburger stand in San Bernandino, California and instead of selling the McDonald brothers his machine, he bought the business; the rest is one of the greatest success stories as Ray Kroc became a pioneer in the fast food industry. He started a uniform system of production for the hamburgers, milk shakes and french fries, so that the food tasted the same in each of the franchises throughout the country and eventually the world. In 1960, Kroc had more than 200 McDonald franchises in the U.S., but he barely earned a profit. He started to prosper when he started the Franchise Realty Corporation which bought up property and leased it to franchisees. With the profits from real estate, Kroc started advertising to support the franchises, and expanded in the 1970's across the globe. From creating an assembly line food production to welcoming ideas from his franchisees, McDonald's has known great success and is often a model for other fast food establishments. Kroc went on to accumulate $500 million dollars in assets.

8. Lew Wallace

At the age of 51 Lew Wallace became the New Mexico Territory governor, from 1878-1881. He was very busy as

---

10 Hubpages.com

governor, but still found time to write. It during his time as governor that he wrote the novel Ben Hur. Wallace was 53 years old when he wrote the novel, and it became the bestselling novel in the 19th century. It has never been out of print.

9. John William Corrington

As a young man, John William Corrington became an English professor after he graduated college. He and his wife wrote several screen plays for movies, including Battle for the Planet of the Apes. When Corrington was 43, he graduated from law school. But after practicing for a few years, at the age of 46 he and his wife became head writers for several soap operas including Search for Tomorrow, General Hospital, Capitol, and several other daytime shows.

10. Tim Zagat

Tim Zagat of the restaurant guide fame, was 44 years old when he started the Zagat Restaurant Guide. When he was 51 years old in 1986, he left his job as a corporate lawyer for Gulf and Western Corporation. Both Tim and his wife Nina were Yale University Law School graduates. Nina, of the same age as her husband, soon left her job as a lawyer to join the company and work with him.

11. Dr. Ruth Westheimer

Dr. Westheimer survived WWII as she was sent to a Switzerland orphanage by her parents who stayed behind in Germany, and were met by the hands of the Nazis. She trained to be a psychologist in France in the 1950's and emigrated to the U.S. She continued her post doctoral education in human sexuality. At 53, she became a household name across the country, for her late night radio-call-in show, fielding questions as a psychosexual therapist. As of 2009, at the age of 81, she was still teaching a few courses at Yale University.

12. Julia Child

Child was 49 years old when her first cookbook, Mastering the Art of French Cooking, was published. At 51 she gained television fame through a cooking show, which premiered in 1963. At the age of 69, she became co-founder of the American Institute of Wine and Food to help advance the knowledge of food and wine through restaurants. In 1984, at the age of 72, she completed the series of 6 videotapes about "The Way to Cook".

13. Peter Mark Roget

Peter Mark Roget was born in 1779. He was a British doctor who was influential in the technology of motion pictures. He was forced to retire, but at the age of 73, published a famous book we still used today. He is best known for Roget's Thesaurus, first known as "Thesaurus of English Words and Phrases Classified and Arranged so as to Facilitate the Expression of Ideas and Assist in Literary Composition". His book has never been out of print since it was published in 1852.

14. Fleming, Florey and Chain

At the age of 47, Sir Alexander Fleming, a British doctor and scientist specialising in studying bacteria discovered penicillin. Years later in 1941, at the age of 43, Howard Florey purified and tested the penicillin vaccine. Ernest Chain was 39, when he created the first large scale production plant to produce penicillin. By 1945, penicillin became commercially available. In 1945, all three men were awarded the Nobel Prize, Fleming was 64, Florey was 47, and Chain was 39.

15. First Gold Medallist

Believe it or not, the oldest Olympic champion won his first and second gold medal when he was 60 years old in 1908 in a deer shooting competition (no deer were actually hurt). He returned to the Olympics in 1912 and won another gold medal. In 1920, he returned again to the Olympics, and won the silver medal, holding the record as the oldest medallist in the Olympics.

16. Benjamin Franklin

Franklin could also be considered a late bloomer, although he did so much in his early life too and has had many success stories. Throughout his years he continued to expand on his genius. He was 46 years old when he experimented with electricity using his kite. At 47, he won the Copley Award, an early version of the Nobel Prize. Between the ages of 47 to 49, he invented bifocals, the catheter, and the Franklin Stove. He was elected to the Continental Congress at age 69. At 70 he signed the Declaration of Independence, making him the eldest signer. When he was 77 years old, he negotiated the Treaty of Paris, which put an end to the Revolutionary War. At 81, he signed the U.S Constitution.

17. Henry Ford

Henry Ford introduced the Model T automobile when he was 45 years old. At the age of 60, he created the first car assembly line.

18. Charles Darwin

Darwin wrote the Origins of Species when he was 50 years old through his years of observing nature.

19. Ramen Noodles

The Japanese businessman Momofuke Ando at the age of 48 invented instant Ramen Noodles with his company, Nissin Foods, which he started 10 years before. Over the years it grew to be a multimillion dollar food company built on dried, fried noodles that he sold in plastic squares and foam cups. In 2005, his instant noodles were taken aboard the Discovery shuttle. Over 100 million people per day eat these products. In 2006, Cup Noodles introduced in 1971 was used by 25 billion people across the globe.

20. Jack Cover

The inventor of the Taser, Jack Cover, was a nuclear physicist. He worked in the aerospace and defence industry supplying parts for the Apollo project run by NASA. He was 50 years old when he started his company, Taser Inc. in 1970. In 1974, he received a patent for his invention which was designed to disable an assailant without using a nonlethal weapon. Today, more than 13,000 law enforcement organisations worldwide, use the taser.

21. Soichiro Honda

Soichiro Honda was 42 years old when he formed the Honda Motor Company in 1948. He created the motorbike by attaching a small engine to a bicycle. The success of that design led him to designing a small motorcycle and within 10 years of starting Honda, he was the leading motorcycle manufacturer in the world. He started manufacturing small engines and cars and the rest is history. In 1988, at the age of 82, he was the first Japanese automobile manufacturer to be included in the Automobile Hall of Fame.

22. Sandra McCauley

At 56, Sandra McCauley went back to school, studying interior design at Canada College in Redwood City, CA. After completing her studies she founded Sandra McCauley Interiors (Carmel, CA) in 2001, bringing her 30 years of experience creating new looks for homes using existing furnishings to the Monterey Peninsula. To succeed in the redesign business McCauley also used her training as an interior designer to provide a more professional and complete product for her clients. Her projects have included whole house remodelling, elder downsizing, organising and storage solutions, staging homes for sale, moving clients into their new homes and many other activities. McCauley is a member of Interior Redesign Industry Specialists (I.R.I.S.). She is involved in her community and is passionate about all her activities, especially her work. Since opening her doors in 2001 she has been a successful Carmel, CA female entrepreneur who's status of 50 plus hasn't impeded her progress.

IT'S NEVER TOO LATE

In some cases, you might think it is too late to pursue your dreams. If you listen to others you can be easily influenced by people who say you are too old to start your own business, to be a writer, or to invent the next great thing. The people who are so often quick to comment why you can't do something probably don't know anything about you regarding your passions and they may not share your dreams. If you wait for permission from someone else you might miss opportunities. You know what you are capable of doing. Don not allow fear of the unknown to stop you, go ahead and take those steps towards what you have always wanted to do. The ordinary and the great among us don't have to be bound by the barrier of age. These "over the hill" success stories are just some of the many people who succeeding in pursuing their dreams later in life. With the right determination, attitude and some luck you can see these people are no different than anyone of us. If you are young, have patience, you have a lot to look forward to achieving. If you are older, go for it now, knowing today is your day and just maybe we will see you at the top.

CHAPTER NINE

'Watch out retirees. Make sure you retire to something
and not from something'.

Ricky K

ENTREPRENEURSHIP IS FUN - YOU ARE YOUR OWN BOSS

You can make it. The only person stopping you is you. The fun of starting life again is what this book highlights. You can be anything you want to be, achieve anything you desire to achieve and attain any height you wish to. It all starts and ends with you. The central idea in starting your own business is to find that which is your passion. Something you enjoy doing can and should be turned into a money making venture, which is one way of ensuring that you will have the verve to wake up every morning looking forward to going to work. Multi billionaire, Sir Richard Branson defines entrepreneurship as *"something that we are born with – because it's about turning what excites us in life into capital so that we can enjoy it even more."*

The Power of the Mind

The human mind has been described as a battlefield. It is the first place where battles of life are won or lost. Research has proved that the same amount of energy it takes to run a race in the mind is the same energy physically required to really run the same race in the body. This only goes to show that if you have been there in the mind, you can get there in your body. All the wonderful ideas and suggestions written in this book will be of no use if you do not believe that they can work for you. It is also important to remember that if you do not believe in yourself or your dreams, others may not believe in you or in your dreams either. So the first step starts with you.

An interesting fact about life is that the principles which govern life are the same for every person, place and time. When applied correctly, the same results are expected. In the event that the results achieved are different, this only means that there is something not being done correctly; there is not a problem with the actual principles. Let' s take the principle of gravity for example. If a person jumps off a cliff, it is irrelevant if they are good or not, the inevitable will happen! The same rule applies with principles of the mind.

This is an important part of life that determines what our actions and results will be. The first place where you as an individual need to make a change or a total overhaul, if necessary, is in your mind.

- What do you think of yourself?
- How do you think about money?
- Are you afraid of failure?
- Are you afraid of success?
- Are you afraid of trying anything at all?

These questions, when answered truthfully, will help you understand wether you are good to go or need to backtrack and 'clean up' your thinking patterns.

There is no magic rule to the way life works. A man only reaps what he sows and not what he wishes he sowed! The principles that govern wealth and success are like peas in a pod and because they are principles, they can be applied in similar situations, location notwithstanding, and the results will be the same. Success is not a respecter of age, class or even religion but simply of principles. These principles will work for anyone who obeys them.

Here are some principles of success that will apply not only in financial success but also in every sphere of life.

Creating and pursuing **SMART** goals

S – Specific Goals
M – Measurable Goals
A – Attainable and Realistic Goals
R – Relevant Goals
T – Time Bound Goals

- Taking decisive and immediate action.
- Making logical and informed decisions.
- Avoiding the trap of trying to make things perfect. (the world does not reward perfectionists, it rewards people who get things done)
- Working outside your comfort zone: Nobody feels 100% ready when opportunities arise, but grabbing the opportunity and working through it ensures a higher chance of success.
- Keeping things simple.
- Focusing on making small, continuous improvement. *"Nothing is perfectly hard if you divide it into small pieces"* - Henry Ford.
- Starting Small.
- Spending time with the right people.
- Maintaining balance in your life.

Oprah Winfrey, who has being described as the wealthiest black woman, has over the years shown great business skills and acumen worthy of emulation. The following are some vital things we can learn from her as a business person who has made a global impact in the world of business and media.

"Forget about the fast lane. If you really want to fly, harness your power to your passion. Honour your calling. Everybody has one. Trust your heart, and success will come to you." - Oprah

1. Discover Your Purpose

According to Oprah, everybody has a calling. And your real job in life is to figure out what it is and get on with the business of doing it. The thing is, once you are truly connected to your purpose in life, the business becomes easy. It's easy to make choices, it's easy to know what to do next (though it is not always so easy to build up the courage to do it!) and it's easy to keep your energy focused on your business. Are you following your true calling?

76

"Let your light shine. Shine within you so that it can shine on someone else. Let your light shine" - Oprah

2. Inspiration sells

Oprah had a genius for keeping her show all about the positive. She never got stuck in the mire like other talk show hosts and dedicated her life to using her platform to inspire and educate others. Some believe that people don't buy feeling good. Oprah has proven this wrong, and shows us that feeling good can sell too! Does your marketing and content make people feel good about themselves?

"If it doesn't feel right, don't do it. That's the lesson. That lesson alone will save you a lot of grief. Even doubt means don't."
- Oprah

3. Be true to yourself

Oprah was constantly barraged with opportunities that did not meet with her focus and objectives for the show. She was approached by numerous people wanting to get on her show. But she was very clear on what did and did not constitute an Oprah show and only did the shows that reflected her values and her brand. By staying true to herself and her values, she was able to keep the quality of her shows high. Are you making compromises in your business that don't feel right? If you have deviated from your initial vision for your business, the best time to retrace your steps is now.

"Surround yourself with only people who are going to lift you higher." - Oprah

4. Use multiple channels

While we may not all have Oprah's budget and reach, we can use the channels that are available to us to spread our good word and work. Oprah used TV, Radio, her website, YouTube, Twitter and her magazine 'O' to effectively spread her message. The great thing about this is that if one way wasn't available or didn't fit with the schedules of her customer base, there were a multitude of others that would. What other channels could you be using to market your business?

"Follow your instincts. That's where true wisdom manifests itself." - Oprah

5. Act quickly when something isn't working

Oprah was warm and engaging on stage, but make no mistake, she was an incredibly savvy business woman and she was quick to make a change when something wasn't working in one of her businesses. Earlier this year, Oprah launched OWN, The Oprah Winfrey Network, a television in partnership with Discovery Networks. When network ratings were slow, the Network head Christina Norman left rather abruptly after only 4 months in the job. Do you make hard decisions quickly in your business?

"When someone shows you who they are, believe them the first time." - Oprah

6. Put YOU into your business

The reason that Oprah had such a long and successful show on TV was because she was real and easy to relate to. She was

78

true to herself in everything that she did and made herself very approachable through her warmth and her ability to connect with her audience. Everyone who watched her show felt like they knew her, like she was their friend. And in many respects she was. How can you put more of yourself into your business? How can you make your clients and colleagues feel like they know the real you? Can they think of you as a friend?

"The big secret in life is that there is no big secret. Whatever your goal, you can get there if you're willing to work." - Oprah

7. Work hard

There is no doubt that Oprah worked hard. In 25 years of taping, she never missed a show, not once! Every day, she would show up at 6:00am, no matter what. It is reported that her executive assistant clocked up over 800 hours of overtime between January and April one year, that's a 12.5 hour work day! If her assistant was putting in this kind of time, you can bet Oprah was putting in more. In the preparation video that Oprah shares on her site, she shares how grateful she is to be able to go out and buy herself a coffee before her meeting that day, and how she is looking forward to spending some time with her friends. In 25 years, Oprah was consumed by her work and it is clear that she would not have achieved the level of success that she did without that dedication to her craft. Could you be putting more into your business? Are there opportunities for extra commitment on your part?

"Do the one thing you think you cannot do. Fail at it. Try again. Do better the second time. The only people who never tumble are those who never mount the high wire. This is your moment. Own it." - Oprah

8. Keep on keeping on

This is the other side of acting quickly when something isn't working. Oprah never sat back and left her fate to the gods. She lived through an atrocious childhood, faced racism and sexism early in her career and yet she still prevailed. She never gave up on her dreams. Success does not happen overnight (as much as we wish it did!), it takes time, effort and showing up. It was these challenges that made Oprah the woman that she is today. These challenges gave her the strength of character, self-determination and resilience that she is known for. Are there areas in your business that could use more focus and persistence?

"Devote today to something so daring even you can't believe you're doing it." - Oprah

9. Be Bold

Oprah committed to everything she did 100%, whether she knew it was going to work or not. One of her great philosophies is that we miss out on life if we don't take risks and she is doing exactly this by leaving her show to focus on her new network. Make no mistake, even for someone of Oprah's stature this is an enormous risk, but an exciting one as well and I am sure that she is looking forward to the challenge that this new venture is giving her.

"I've come to believe that each of us has a personal calling that's as unique as a fingerprint – and that the best way to succeed is to discover what you love and then find a way to offer it to others in the form of service, working hard, and also allowing the energy of the universe to lead you." - Oprah

80

10. Leave them wanting more

Oprah retired from her show at the top of her game. She could have easily continued for years, very successfully, but instead she decided to leave while her show was still the number one daytime talk show in the USA. Oprah knew her time had come and decided to step down while she was still at the top. This allowed her to focus on her other ventures and move onto the next stage in her life. By making herself less available on regular TV, she will use her new channel to maintain her presence in people's lives. How best can you use your business to touch the lives of people around you and make an impact in your environment?

MORE ENTREPRENEURIAL SUCCESS TIPS FROM COLONEL SANDERS

[11]Despite the unfortunate turn of events near the end of his life Colonel Sanders died in 1980, age 90 — there are still some gems in his autobiography on dealing with life's curveballs, honing your entrepreneurial spirit and simply enjoying work life more.

Learn to love work

Back in 1900, at the age of 10, Sanders got his first job working on a farm to support his widowed mother and family of four. It didn't last long, in Sanders's own words: "There were bluebirds and red squirrels and other things that attracted a boy's interest and I didn't clear as much ground as I ought to have cleared." Sanders got fired, and when he arrived home with two dollars, naturally, his mother was furious. He decided from there on out, he would aim to satisfy his employers — put in enough hours and do enough work.

His second employer was a German farmer called Henry Monk. In an effort to redeem himself with his mother, Sanders worked hard on Monk's farm and discovered that he loved the rush of accomplishment. Saying of hard work: *"once you get used to it, there's great pleasure in working hard."*

It's important to take stock of your accomplishments, celebrate them, and use them as fuel while you work towards other milestones. Loving work is easy when you see it as a conduit for accomplishments. We have a "Board of Awesomeness" at Memeburn. Every now and again we stick an accomplishment on it — like getting SEO'ed to the top spot for the term "Google tricks." It feels good to glance at that board on hard days.

---

11 www.ventureburn.com – '6 Finger Licking Good Tips For Success From Colonel Sanders'

"I've never believed in holding back or stinting on anything I've ever done and I've only had two rules: Do all you can, and do it the best you can. It's the only way you ever get the feeling of accomplishing something," wrote Sanders.

Don't be afraid to change your career

Before Sanders became the Colonel, he had a whole bunch of disparate jobs. He was an army mule-tender, locomotive fireman, railroad worker, insurance salesman, amateur obstetrician and a ferryboat entrepreneur. It was only when he was offered the lease of a gas and service station that his destiny as the founder of KFC began to take shape. Sanders was 65 years old when he began franchising KFC. "Don't quit at age 65, maybe your boat hasn't come in yet, mine hadn't," he said in an interview. Keep looking until you find something you love, you'll probably excel at it.

Add value wherever you can

What do your customers expect from your product or service? Now, add a little bit extra. For example, when Sanders took over the Standard Oil service station, the locals in town refused to buy fuel from the new guy in town. Sanders had to figure out a way to make the locals like him. *"I remembered travelling around selling tyres, and one place had given me the kind of service I had never gotten elsewhere. They had wiped my windshield. It was that simple,"* said Sanders.

People expected fuel for their cars and what they got was not only a windshield wash, but Sanders went a step further and filled up their tyres. People came from all over, to experience a full service station. The station's sales tripled to a new record.

Unfortunately, Sanders's business went bankrupt in the late 1920s , just as the Depression was starting a severe drought hit Kentucky. Farmers couldn't pay their credit at the service station. Sanders's reputation preceded him however, and Shell offered him a station rent free if he agreed to relocate to Corbin Kentucky.

This is where the story of KFC began. When a truck driver mentioned that there was nowhere good to eat in the area, Sanders saw an opportunity to add value.

Start simple and do simple well

Following his aforementioned ethos of "do all you can, and do it best you can," Sanders put his simple, homemade cooking skills to good use. He set up his own dining room table and six chairs in a room attached to the service station and started serving hot meals to hungry customers. There were no menus, no choices, just quality food.

The word got out and Sanders approach of selling complementary items, fuel and food worked a treat. Sanders advertised by painting signs on barns within 150 miles of Corbin. Sanders wrote that one driver followed signs for 200 miles. "I thought I'd find a 12-storey building when I got here." Of course Sanders's setup was considerably smaller, but it offered quality food — the most important thing. It didn't matter that the Sanders's fledgling business was modest, when the hungry driver dug into the food, the advertising seemed completely warranted.

In 1936 Sanders was granted the status of honorary Colonel by the Kentucky governor for his contributions to the state's cuisine. By 1937 the restaurant had grown to 142 seats.

Take an interest in technology and experiment

Fried chicken wasn't on the Colonel's menu originally; it took too long to cook. In 1939 the pressure cooker was introduced and before long Sanders started experimenting with cooking fried chicken. He succeeded of course. By 1940 he had perfected his secret recipe of 11 herbs and spices and he could cook fresh, fried chicken in under eight minutes. Be on the lookout for new technologies and how their innovative uses can potentially boost your business.

Don't be afraid to get your hands dirty

12 years later, Sanders introduced his fried-chicken to a friend, Pete Harman in Salt Lake City. He cooked the fried chicken for Harman and his wife himself, in the hope that Harman would sell the chicken at his restaurant. Harman didn't make any promises, but did a test run. It turned out to be a hit with his patrons and so Harman agreed to sell the Colonel's chicken permanently. Harman's restaurant became the first KFC franchise.

Three years later life threw Sanders another curve ball. A new interstate highway meant that Corbin would no longer be a prominent stop for truck drivers. At the age of 65, Sanders sold his service station on an auction and started collecting social security cheques. Funded by only his cheques, the Colonel set off on a mission to sell franchises across the country and cooked meals for restaurant owners himself as he went. Some shunned him, while others welcomed him, but he persisted and took it upon himself to make his business succeed. The Colonel also personally trained his original franchisees on how to cook the chicken. That was one way he could be sure the quality would not wane.

CHAPTER TEN

YOU CAN MAKE IT. THE TIME TO START IS NOW

YOU CAN MAKE IT

Retirement is your prime time to live out your dreams and follow your passions. If there is something you care about passionately, you have your inspiration. Think also about the dreams you held at various times in your life. You might have pushed aside important dreams because they were impractical at the time. Ask yourself if those dreams still matter to you? Do they spark excitement when you think about them? If they do, you have found your inspiration. Now is the time to do that which you have wanted to do for a very long time. Take the bull by the horns and achieve your dream.

Business ideas for 50+ entrepreneurs

Starting up can be characterised by lots of adrenaline and zest which may die down at the first sign of a hurdle or challenge. Here are some truths we need to establish before venturing into any business.

- Building a business takes time. Be realistic in your income goals and expectations. If you need a steady income right now to pay your rent or feed your children, then it's unlikely that you can do that by starting a business now.

- Don't try to be all things to all people. It's not uncommon to think that the more products or services you offer the more potential customers you have. By specialising, you can focus your marketing efforts more successfully and you can become known as the "go-to person" or expert for a particular product or service. Once you make a success of one business, you can always add others later.

- Do something you enjoy. It's easier to sustain the necessary motivation and commitment if you like what you're doing.

[12]BEST PROFITABLE SMALL BUSINESS START UP IDEAS FOR RETIREES

1. Start a consultancy business based on your expertise The job position you held before retirement is not key, you can start a consultancy business around any career field or profession. For instance, if you retired as an accountant; you could become a chartered private auditor or become a financial adviser. If you were a marketer, you could become a marketing consultant. In fact, the business consultancy ideas are limitless. Just analyse your present skills and you can build a thriving consultancy business around it.

2. Start a professional public speaking service business
If business consultancy is not the way to go for you, then you can sell your expertise or knowledge on platforms. You could become a professional speaker; leveraging your job experience and acquired skills. Your subject line is limitless, all you need do is to identify a need and add a little touch of creativity.

3. Start a blog based on your expertise
Take the approach of starting a consultancy business and bring it online. You just need to start a blog. Starting a blog costs little or next to nothing but the potential is great.

4. Start a network marketing business

5. Start an online training class based on your experience

6. Start a home based tutoring service business

7. Start an information research business

8. Start a lawn care business

9. Start a mini day care centre

10. Start a babysitting service business

11. Start a pet sitting business
Do you enjoy looking after animals? Many people have pets but are too busy to look after them or provide them with the attention and care they need on a daily basis.

12. Start a mail order business

13. Start a crafts exporting business

---

14. Start a poultry business
15. Start a catfish rearing business
16. Start a freelance writing business
17. Start a magazine or newsletter publishing business
18. Start an event planning business
19. Start a janitorial service business (office cleaning)
[13]20. Start a business selling used books
21. Start a mini fitness training centre
22. Start a tutorial centre on anything e.g. web design, crafts, hair dressing, etc
23. Start a babysitting service business
24. Start a hair braiding business
25. Start a barber shop or salon in your neighbourhood
26. Start a private process server business
27. Start a website building business

Websites are big business because every viable and reputable business needs one but not everyone has the know-how. A good, functioning website that is easy to use for the customer can often be the key ingredient to a successful business.

28. Start a mobile detailing business
29. Start a mobile phone repair centre

Almost everyone has a mobile phone and with phone contracts lasting 12-24 months people often opt to have their damaged phones repaired rather than take out insurance or purchase a new phone.

30. Start a mobile bookshop business

If books are a passion for you then this could be a suitable start-up business. With the internet people can purchase the
majority of things they desire from the comfort of their own home, why not continue with that trend and provide a bookshop that goes to the customer?

31. Start a mobile library
32. Start a poultry business
33. Start a janitorial business
34. Start an internet based business

Here are some steps you can take In order to start selling your personal items on eBay:

- Get yourself registered on eBay as a seller.
- Set up your own Paypal account to receive payments.
- Look around your house and garage and identify the unused items that you would like to sell.
- List your items for sale on eBay, sit back and watch the auctions. Once the auctions are complete, collect the payment and send the items to the buyer promptly and as described. Don't forget to get feedback from the buyer.
- Most people nowadays have had a go at buying or selling items on eBay. Anyone can list anything from their unwanted clothing to their grandmother's antiques. However, some eBay sellers take things a step further and turn their eBay transactions into a business whereby they not only earn money whilst decongesting their own home, they actively seek out things to sell on eBay too.

CONCLUSION

In a nutshell starting a business at 50+ could not be easier:

- Retiring does not necessarily mean the end, it can and should mean the start of something new.
- The characteristics of those 50+ lean towards traits that benefit the entrepreneur mindset.
- There are similarities between self-employment and becoming an entrepreneur, in-fact the two are the same thing provided that the self-employed person positions themselves to take the same risks as the entrepreneur. You can start with a desire to become your own boss and grow your company and vision from there. Don't get comfortable, it's important to think BIG!
- There are many positives to starting your own

business. Your time is yours to manage and you have complete autonomy over everything that happens within your company. You are in control.

- There are countless stories of people who have started successful businesses later in life; use them as inspiration, understanding that if it was possible for someone else to achieve then it is also possible for you.
- Discover and identify your passion, then through research and brainstorming find a viable business that links your passion to a profit making entity; be it a service you provide or a product you offer.
- Remember to have fun. This season of your life is about following your passions and discovering what truly drives you. Your business idea must relate to something that you enjoy, admire and care about. It must be based on something that evokes a spark within you.

The key to becoming an entrepreneur can be found in two things; your mindset and your determination. You must make a quality decision and stick to it. Even if things do not initially appear to go as you envisaged, you must have a dogged and tenacious attitude that says you will never give up.

Regret is one of the most despairing things in life. To look back at your life 20 years from now and have a pool of regrets or 'if only's' is not desirable. Do not wait until tomorrow, that is the process of someone who procrastinates and plans but never takes action. Avoid any further delay and begin today. Get a notebook and pen and start to jot down your dreams, ideas and visions for your future business. Entrepreneurs are not just visionaries and dreamers, they do not merely plan. Entrepreneurs are people of action. So with everything you jot down, make sure that you actually start doing. Don't simply have a notebook filled with ideas that go no further than your coffee table.

Remember, your age can work in your favour, focus on the positives; the years of experience you bring, the life-skills you possess and the wisdom you have acquired over the years are valuable assets. Use them to your advantage. The only real obstacle you have in your way is you! Once you have purposed in your heart and determined to become an entrepreneur, no one can stop you. Why not live life to the full? Experience an enriched, satisfying life that is fulfilled as you embark upon a journey of success as a true entrepreneur!

Appendix 1:

Here are some business ideas you can choose from to help set you on the path to entrepreneurship.

List of Business Ideas/Consulting Services

Agricultural consultant Air quality consultant
Coach (personal or business) or mentor
Computer Consultant
Construction management consultant
Diversity consultant
Engineering consultant
Environmental consultant
Expert witness
Failure evaluation Franchise consultant Healthcare consultant Human resources consultant Image consultant
International consultant
Marketing consultant
Medical office consultant
Product development consultant
Proposal consultant (government contracts)
Proposal consultant (grants) Retail consultant
Risk management consultant Safety consultant
Total quality management consultant
Training consultant
Utility auditing consultant

Retail and commercial

Antique shop Bar/Club
Used book store Bicycle sales
Books Boutique owner
Calligraphy Chemicals Chinese food take-out service Clothing Store
Coffee shop owner Craft broker
Craft supplies catalog
eBay Business Fishing supplies
Gift Basket service
Handmade soap Homemade foods

Online Business Pizza parlour Posters
Restaurant and food business Sewing crafts
Stamps Tapes
Used books Wood crafts

Consumer and business services

Advertising specialty sales Appliance repair
Audio tape duplication Bed and Breakfast Inn Bicycle repair
Bulletin board sysop Business plan writer Business plan writing Cabinet maker
Car Detailing
Carpet and upholstery Catering
Chemical testing Child Care Service Chimney sweep
Cleaning Service Clown
Coin dealer Collectibles dealer Collections service
Concrete construction and repair Cook
Cosmetologist
Crafts instructor Currency auctions Dance instructor
Daycare for adults Dental claims processing Directory publishing Disk duplication
Electrician
Employment agency Environmental cleanup service Errand service
Executive recruiter Financial planner

94

Janitorial supplies
Jewellery
Mail order business
Consumer and business services
Framing service (picture frames)
Genealogist
Grant writer Hair
Salon
Handyman services Home
automotive Tuneup
service
Home or office organisation services
Home Design service
Housekeeper Information
broker Inventory control
service Janitorial service
Landscaping
Laundry service Lawn
cutting
Lawnmower and motor repair
Limousine service
Loan consultant
Locksmith
Magician Mailing
service Market
research Medical
Claims billing Medical
transcription Moving
company Novelty
T-shirt sales Painter
Personal fitness trainer
Personal Concierge Pet
sitting
Pet walking Pet
grooming
Pet waste cleanup
Plumber
Pool cleaning service
Portrait and wedding photography
Re-modelling service
Seminar producer Screen
printing Shopping
Service
Shuttle service Re-modelling service
Seminar producer
Screen printing Shopping
Service Shuttle service
Computer & Internet

Flea market seller
Sightseeing tours
Small business consultant
Swimming pool maintenance Tax
preparation Telemarketing service
Telephone service reseller Tool
rental
Translation service Travel
Agency Tutor
TV repair VCR
repair
Video   duplication
Window cleaning Yard
cleanup

Editorial & graphic design
Novelist Proofreader
Publicist
Search engine optimization
Subscription newsletter Translator
Web designer
Web content provider Write audio
cassette scripts Write book jacket
blurbs Write company histories
Write Publicity Releases
Nonfiction writer
Newsletter production for clients

Office services
Business Support Service
Desktop Publishing
Bookkeeping Commercial art
Legal transcription Mailing list
management Medical
transcription Resume writing
Virtual Assistant

Entertainment
Agent
Ballet studio

Computer consulting Computer
repair
Computer disk back up services
Computer programming Computer
training
Search engine optimisation
Search Engine Marketing
Web site development Web
site hosting

Sales

Manufacturer's sales representative
Network Marketing
Telemarketing service
Sales coach or trainer Advertising
specialties
Direct selling
Printer toner recharging

Planning and organising businesses

Business plan writing
Business turnarounds
Closet organising Event
Planning service
Meeting planning Party
Planning
Show promoting
Wedding consultant

Band leader Dance
company Dancer
One-man band Singer
Song writer

Automotive Automobile
detailing Auto parts sales
Auto repair garage
Brake replacement & repair Car wash
Junk car removal Muffler shop

Miscellaneous services
Environmental restoration Fund
raiser Import/Export business
Plant nursery (raise and sell house plants and
annuals)
Raising and racing horses

Appendix 2:

Aptitude Test

Instructions: Read each question and pick the answer that most accurately describes your behaviour, feeling or attitude as it actually is, not as you would like it to be or think it should be. You must be honest with yourself to get a valid score.

STATEMENT	YES	NO
I welcome change.		
I know myself well.		
I always finish whatever I undertake.		
I am sociable.		
I am well organised.		
I am not afraid of work, even if I know that it will take an undetermined amount of time before I can measure the results.		
I am not afraid of making decisions, even if I know I might make a mistake.		
I can take criticism, even if ill-intentioned. I adjust, if necessary, but I forge on.		

Now think deeply. Here are more statements to ponder.

STATEMENT	YES	NO
When I know I'm right, I like to convince others, and generally succeed in doing so.		
I like to challenge myself in sports, but do not like team sports.		
I believe money is a good indicator of success.		
I know what I am capable of, and I like taking on new challenges enthusiastically. I am generally realistic and reasonably optimistic about the results.		
Success is a matter of will power and self discipline. Whatever happens to me is the result of my own actions, or inactions.		
I can communicate my enthusiasm easily, and win people over to my cause.		
I look forward to knowing the results of my actions, and I make sure to find out.		
I like to take calculated risks in life.		
I am confident that I will succeed, when I undertake something difficult.		
I can do many things at once, and can solve problems quickly.		

Finally, for some challenging questions without which your aptitude test will not be complete.

STATEMENT	YES	NO
Obstacles are made to be overcome. They are a source of opportunities.		
I dislike inactivity. I like to keep busy, doing something constructive, even in my leisure activities.		
I like doing things my way, even if it means doing things very differently.		
I like to plan my moves, when the outcome is important to me. In fact, I believe I could not succeed without a well thought out plan.		
Unforeseen events spur me on. I find them challenging.		
Success is the result of planning, sustained efforts, and hard work. Luck generally has little to do with it.		
I take pleasure in transforming uncertainty into manageable situations.		
Long term commitment is key to reaching my goals.		
I can concentrate on what I am doing. I can work long hours, and lose track of time.		
I derive intense pleasure in achieving what others generally think impossible.		
I am a motivated, patient individual.		
I like being my own boss.		

Had enough? You have arrived at the moment of truth. This test will give you a useful heads-up on your suitability for entrepreneurship.

[14]**Add the number of "Yes" answers together** to reveal your readiness to start your own business. These are rough estimations which will require further investigation. Use the answers as a general guide only!

30 to 27: You are likely an entrepreneur already! If not, you are wasting precious quality time. Meanwhile, your employer is very fortunate to have you!

26 to 20: You have the profile of an entrepreneur. You can succeed on your own. Do investigate further.

19 to 14 : You have the potential to become an entrepreneur. However, there are still some aspects that you are not comfortable with. You should definitely investigate yourself further, before attempting to go off on your own.

13 to 9 : You are a borderline entrepreneur. You can become one, if you really work on yourself. Seek the help of a professional coach, to start you off on the right foot.

8 or less : Obviously, you will have to work with a partner who will complement your aptitudes and ability. You should think things through thoroughly before going off on your own. Seek professional guidance to help you in your decision.

14 Free Aptitude Tests for Entrepreneurs at http://Free Aptitude Tests For Aspiring Entrepreneurs.html

Appendix 3:

Market Study

(How do you know your business idea is the right one? Answer the following questions to the best of your ability. If you do not know the answers, talk to people who run similar businesses).

1. Describe your industry (what are its key features? Is it seasonal – a cyclical business - or simply all year round? Is it experiencing explosive growth right now?):

2. Describe the size of the market opportunity:

3. Who are your competitors? Would you be able to access a share of the market? Or is the market saturated?:

4. What are your major competitors' products and/or services?:

5. How do they obtain their raw materials for their products and services?:

6. Based on an estimate of your competitors, how much revenue could you expect to earn from your business in your first month, six months, or one year?

7. How do your competitors reach their customers? Would the same methods work for you?

Appendix 4:

Marketing Plan
(Fill in the marketing template below using the example as a guide)

Product / Service	Features	Benefits	Target Audience	Advertising Strategy	Costs
Dry-cleaning	Use of non-bleaching, hypo-allergenic detergents to wash customers' clothes in order to preserve colour and beauty.	Good for suits, formal wear, and children's clothes	Working adults and mothers	Word of mouth, fliers distributed in neighbour-hoods and radio spot	N10,000 initially

Appendix 5:

Business Plan Template
(Your business plan should include the following sections especially if you intend to obtain a loan. Fill in the blank spaces).

Executive Summary (Write this after you have written all the other sections. It is simply a summary of your business concept):

Business Description (What is your company established to do?)

Products and Services (What would you be offering the public and in what format?)

Marketing Plan (How do you plan to sell your products? Refer to Appendices 1 and 2):

Management and Personnel (How would you run your business?):

Financial Investment Data (What funds would you need to start and where do you plan to get your funding? How would you continue to invest capital into your business?):

Financial Plan (Paint a larger picture of your day-to-day expenses beyond your initial start up costs):

Appendices (attach other important documents):

Purchase all the books within the *Entrepreneurial Development Series.* They are available online and in bookstores near you.

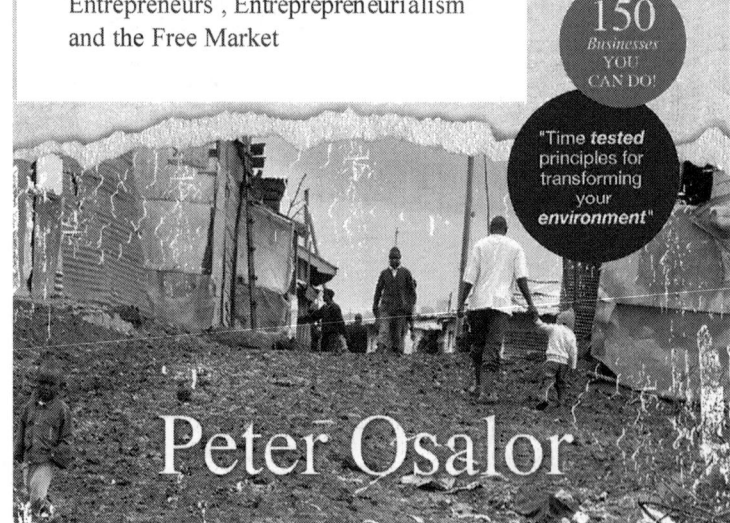

50 Proven

Cures

For Poverty

Entrepreneurs , Entreprepreneurialism
and the Free Market

150
Businesses
YOU
CAN DO!

"Time *tested*
principles for
transforming
your
environment"

Peter Osalor

The Entrepreneurial Revolution

A solution for poverty eradication

Peter Osalor FCCA, CTA

III

teenage

Entrepreneurs

The **Best** Time To Start Your Own Business

100+
Businesses
TEENAGERS
CAN DO'

Peter Osalor

Women
Empowerment
& Entrepreneurial
Revolution

The solution for a prosperous society, poverty eradication and wealth creation

r05alor

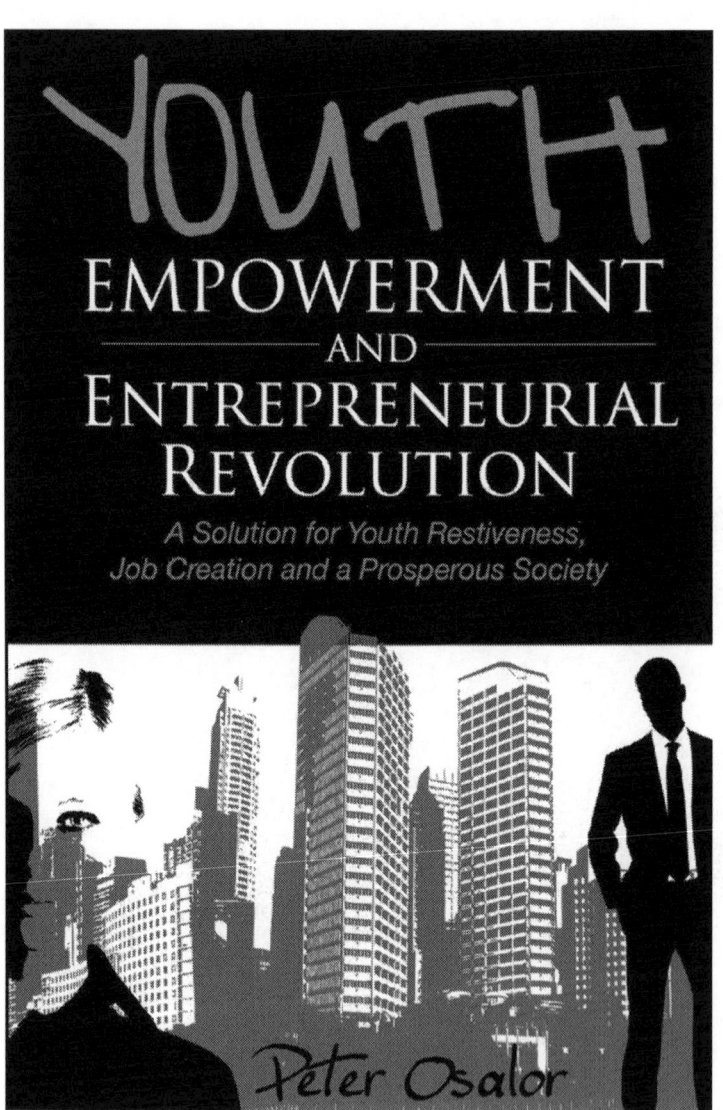

Peter Osalor

ECONOMIC
TRANSFORMATION

*From a Poor Person to a Wealthy Person,
From a Poor Nation to a Wealthy Nation*

Entrepreneur, Entrepreneurship, Entrepreneulism,
MSME, Entrepreneurial Revolution

COMING SOON

12214362R00066

Printed in Great Britain
by Amazon.co.uk, Ltd.,
Marston Gate.